GW00692057

Gallery Books
Editor Peter Fallon

GOING BY WATER

Michael Coady

GOING BY WATER

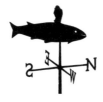

Gallery Books

Going by Water
is first published
simultaneously in paperback
and in a clothbound edition
on 22 November 2009.

The Gallery Press
Loughcrew
Oldcastle
County Meath
Ireland

www.gallerypress.com

ISBN 978 1 85235 484 8 *paperback*
     978 1 85235 485 5 *clothbound*

A CIP catalogue record for this book
is available from the British Library.

Contents

So we beat on, boats against the current, borne back ceaselessly into the past.
— F Scott Fitzgerald, *The Great Gatsby*

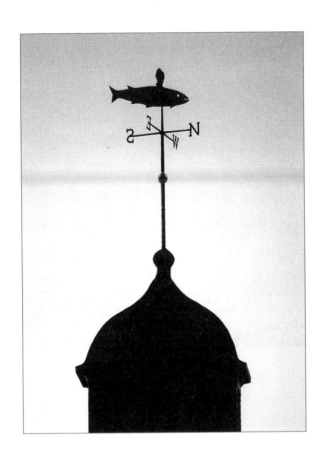

Morning Bell

Six on the town clock strikes through winter dark
above the huddled roofs, the streets and lanes,
the pillowed heads and dreams, the tiding river.

So many loose ends left to be lived out
on this settled ground long overlain
with lives and days dissolved in mystery

where the sleepers and the dead are in the dark
as each hour marks an end and a beginning.
What comes now with countdown to first light?

The same again, the old bell says — the roofs,
the pillowed heads, the dreams, the tides — the same
but not the same, this winter morning here.

PART ONE

Sister River

Boys are fishing from a bridge
built before Columbus raised a sail.

What lasts is what you start with.
— Charles Wright,
'A Journal of Southern Rivers'

Leac na Tine

Flagstone of the Fire

*Summer and harvest the driest ever remembered. Very little rain
from May to the 5th of November. Grinding of wheat became so
difficult for want of water that . . . bread was hard to be procured
in Carrick.*
    — James Ryan, diarist, 1803

Rivermen say that in rare times
of longest drought and lowest tide,
when the submerged flagstone in midstream
below the ancient bridge was bared,
cotsmen of Carrick used to vie
to light a fire upon it, and so
a perennial marker under water
came to be known as *Leac na Tine.*

No one living now has viewed
the stone's emergence into air
although we've watched and waited for it
through hot summers and seen it almost
surface during heatwaves we half
forget and half remember, along with
floods and frosts and hurricanes,
all the weather gone downriver.

A fisherman I know explains
that long ago the tides were different,
and summers warmer, and quaysides
not yet built when his grandfather's
great-grandfather last stood
on the flagstone and lit the fire
in midstream, and that he heard
it looked from farther off
as if the water itself had taken fire

and was challenging the sky
to muster clouds, restore the river.

And then I recognize this comes
out of deep time:
                    rain-making ritual
and submerged parable revealing
how elements that seem unlinked
are all essentially conjoined —

fire and water,
            earth and air,
sun and rain
            and fields of corn,
river flow
            and millwheels turning,
hands in flour
            and ovens fired,
fresh bread
            upon the table.

Finding a Name

No one remembers
a name for the streamlet
joining the river above Poll Saillí,
the pool of the willows.

Cast off your shoes like a child
and step into the flow
to find the way,
back through the current

and course of the years
by the reeds and stones,
by the bracken,
the ash and the rowan,

by the grassy path and the hazel
to a place of briars and nettles
and mossed-over stones
beside a bare gable

where once before dawn
in a room at the head of the stairs
by a window that faced
the brow of a hill to the east

time came
for breaking of waters,
for blood
and first cry.

By noon the name
Abigail had been given
with candle and water and word,
and by nightfall

as darkness deepened
the turn of the flow
under leaves of the alder
she'd left her last

breath on the air,
light as a wisp of down
from the breast
of a wren or a dove.

Stand barefoot in water
there and utter
the name Abigail
that's carried away

on the face of the ripple
still joining the river
above Poll Saillí,
the pool of the willows.

June Impromptu

Drifting on the tide from Town Pond to Ormond Castle
I'm sitting in with a local ensemble
of sky and valley, river, cot and paddle
making up a rhapsody of now
extemporized in riffs from dogs and blackbirds,
children's shouts and laughter from the bridge,
dip and swirl of water as I paddle,
and a helicopter rapping over Slievenamon.

Under all, or over, photosynthesis
fine-tunes the world, unheard, in every leaf.
All of this flows on towards a cadence
deeper than surrender of the drowned —
some replete and consummate observance
which for Simone Weil was prayer and praise.

Stitching the Bridge

for James

At full tide on a summer evening
man and boy
father and son
the boy in the bow, the man behind

crossing the river in a cot
timing paddle strokes and turns
in a game they've made
on the tidal swell

of making for
the other side
by weaving through
every arch in turn

deftly lining in and out
upstream and down
through narrow turns
without scraping wood

against the ancient bridge of stone
that holds what's given
and all that's lost
in the silted story of the town.

The boy will remember
in days to come
when he's a man,
his father gone;

other fathers in their blood
knew this crossing in their turn.

Talitha Cumi

And he took the damsel by the hand, and said unto her, Talitha cumi; which is, being interpreted, Damsel, I say unto thee, arise.
— Mark 5.41, King James version

They were searching for the little one all the way from where she went in on the Carrick Mór side to as far down as Roche's Quay in Tinhalla. But without sign or light of her.

The mother and father were demented and my aunt Katie was trying to console them. She put on her Sunday coat and hat and headed across the Old Bridge up to the Friary in Carrick Beg. There was a friar there with a name for healing and for searches in the river. He was supposed to be fond of the drop as well. He had the look of a man tormented.

Himself and Katie bound a sheaf of the straw that had been kept from the crib of the previous Christmas. Then the friar took the sheaf and went out with the fishermen. He was wearing the brown habit, with the hood, and the rope knotted around his waist. He took off his sandals and stepped barefoot into one of the cots. We'll go out now in the name of God, he said.

It was the third day of searching. My father brought me along with him. I was fifteen or sixteen and handy on the river. And he thought I was lucky at fishing. He was starting to have trouble with his eyes at the time and coming to rely on me to paddle when the men went out to make a haul.

We waited until the floodtide was slowing the current and covering the town weir. Then the friar fixed a blessèd candle on a small wooden cross bound into the sheaf. He said a Latin prayer and let the sheaf with the lighted candle out on the flow where the child had fallen in, above Boreen na gCapall.

We followed along in the cots, just dipping our paddles to stay with the drift, through the Town Pond between the two bridges and down past Tobar na gCrann. Just when we thought the candle was about to burn out the sheaf of straw floated in beside one of the sally islands below the castle and stopped. And I swear to God, there she was, just under the surface, caught in overhanging sallies. A pale little face turned up to us, rising and sinking in a swirl of backwater.

The men lifted the poor child, blessing themselves in dread. There was scarcely a mark on her. And the friar was sitting in the cot in his robes and bare feet, holding her in his arms as if she was only asleep, and chanting the one thing over and over. It sounded like Tell it and come, tell it and come. There was a strange tone in his voice that never left my head.

He laid the child down in his lap and started to wash some mud from her little hands. She was wearing a blouse or bodice that was oozing water. Then, as true as God is my judge, all of a sudden the blouse stirred and a white trout rose out of it, and jumped clean over the gunnel of the cot, back into the river.

It shook us all, and the friar more than anyone. He drew the hood up over his head and started moaning to himself, leaning down over the little girl. A thing I never saw before or since: a priest crying.

After a while he steadied himself and started praying, Hail holy queen, Mother of mercy, Hail our life, our sweetness and our hope.

We turned the cots upriver to bring the child back home on the tide.

The Friars' Rock

We come to rivers when we are young or old.
— Derek Mahon, 'Waterfront'

The boulder deep midstream
has never shown itself in air
nor shifted since the glacier
dropped it there
twelve thousand years ago
where in immeasurable
course of flowing seasons, floods and tides,
in human time when Joan of Arc
was still a child,
Franciscan monks arrived
to build a salmon weir
upstream of the rock

and in their generations
swimmers out beyond their depth
on lost summer days
stood up in mid-flow
when they found footing
as they still do
on that hidden mark
that's settled there

still bedded
in the flow
and rooted
beyond time
within the dreaming
heads of all who've ever
come and swam and gone
or still live on
beside the sister river.

The Feast of Saint Nicholas

Wind rises in the night,
growls and whines, then holds
its breath, as though
pretending it's said all
it means to say.

Across the river
a man lies sleepless,
listening to the dark
breath on the water
and its tidings,

hands crossed on his breast,
seeking to grip
the shadow within.

Easter tide

Voices off the River

I NEW YEAR'S EVE

*i.m. Bernadette Quehen and her children, Alain,
Nathalie, Bernard and Mary, who died in the
river Suir at Carrick-on-Suir, 31 December 1979*

That sunny morning after hard frost
on the last day of the year
I had just gone down the town
for bread and milk and the paper
when I heard the news
going through the place like a knife —

the car, the mother and children
gone into the flood after slipping
from Carrick Beg quay.

Half of the town was rushing
to crowd on to the bridge and quays.
The sight of a little slipper
left on the floor of a boat
was enough to bring tears

with the people's grief becoming
blind anger that turned
on the heart of things —

people who live by a river
helplessly raging
against the flowing
force that brought
their settlement into being.

Nothing worse than this
had ever happened

in the memory of those still living
although this place,
two hundred years back, had seen
scores of terrified women
and children drown within minutes
when their boat capsized in a raging
flood at that bridge.

In time in a time
this morning's story also
would be buried
and almost forgotten
along with its tears,
for that is our only way
to go on living.

That frosty morning of New Year's Eve
the sun shone down
on women and men
gathered in grief,
their tears flowing together
by the river and the bridge,

while four swans in alarm
beat up off the water,
rose above quays and houses
and circled high over
the human commotion,
then headed upriver
towards Dovehill.

2 WHAT PADDY DOHERTY REMEMBERS MUNDY HAYDEN TELLING

They were coming back
after making a haul
when he heard
the voice of a woman
humming and singing
out on the river

and then they saw her
in the half-light
coming along,

sitting up and floating
on the water, her clothes
ballooned around her
and keeping her up
as she hummed along
to herself on the tide —

the mind gone on her
when she went in.

They pulled across
in the cots
and humoured her home
while she was still
humming away
a song her father
used to sing to her
when she was young.

3 TITANIC

The man who lived
in the house that used to be
there in Oven Lane
was called Titanic because
he was supposed to sail on her
out from Queenstown
to meet up with the brother
in New York

but had no stomach for it
on the morning he was to go
on account of the big farewell
of the night before.

4 THE WOBBLER'S TALE

He swore
by the holy jingos
and the high cross
of Kilkenny

that his father was all
his life on the river
but couldn't
swim a stroke —

lost his balance
once in the cot,
and took a header
into the tide,

then walked
underwater
to get to the bank

and surfaced
with a salmon
in his arms.

5 DREAM COUNTRY

She dreamed
that she dived
one summer's evening
from the bridge

and into a full tide —
then turned underwater
and kicked back up
to light and air

to find herself
in another place,
another time.

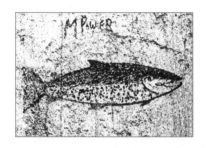

6 THE STRANGER

We were out for most of the night
after making three or four hauls
without a pull of a fish.

Before dawn we drew into the island
to light a fire and boil up the tea
before packing it in.

A man stepped out of the dark
and into the light of the fire,
standing over us
like he owned the place.

Any luck with the fishing? he asked
and we said, No, not a thing.
Try it again, he said,
as soon as the light
shows over the hill —
two hours ago in the Long Reach
fish were breaking in shoals
on the first of the flood.

Sure enough we put out again
and met up with a big flock of salmon
that threatened to sink the cots.
We dragged a few netfuls in on the mud
and had to get help in bringing them home.

I think the count was fifty-three.
John Toms the Waterford buyer said
the likes of that haul of salmon
seldom, if ever, was seen.

We never found out who the stranger was
who was gone as quick as he came.
My brother Tommy was inclined to believe
he wasn't a flesh and blood man
but maybe one of the boatload of all
the women and children and soldiers lost
long ago on a raging flood
after a blizzard of sleet and snow

when the barge bringing more than a hundred
down from Clonmel
tried to pull in above the town
but swung sideways-on in the torrent
and couldn't be stopped
till it whirled around and tipped over,
then shattered with all the people
against the bridge.

They say the bodies
and ghosts and bones
of all those drowned
were coming to light
below in the islands
for years.

7 THE SCALES OF THE SALMON

for Eugene O'Callaghan

There was no fishing that early spring
on account of the floods that lasted beyond
St Patrick's Day. Cupboards were bare

but my grandfather Dan wouldn't throw in the towel
so word came to the house to be out for a haul
one morning at seven above the New Bridge.

My father was sick so I had to go
before school in his place, along with Dan,
old Paddy Meagher and Paddy Foran.

Making the haul that morning
the water was terrible strong
and it looked like we'd have to give in —

but then old Dan pulled on
the net ropes with a grunt
and was drawing in two big salmon.

They were so powerful he had to wrestle them
down on the floor of the cot. One was
twenty-nine pounds, the other twenty-seven.

When they were killed and Dan raised his head
I started to laugh to see his moustache
and chin all covered in scales —

I can see it still —

and as I looked on I also took in
my uncle Willmo just then above us
crossing the bridge on his way to work.

Willmo looked down and saw the cots,
the men and the fish, old Dan with the salmon
scales decorating his face

and myself,
the young fellow,
laughing.

That morning we were all thankful to God
as we pulled into the bank
below the bridge.

I doused my face
in Tobar na gCrann,
then headed off, a bit late for school.

In the years to come
my grandfather Dan
went blind as a bat
but still fished on.

Going by Water

i.m. William O'Callaghan, 1925-2006

. . . river teach me stubbornness and endurance
so in the last hour I become worthy
of rest in the shade of the delta
in the holy triangle of the beginning and the end.
> — Zbigniew Herbert, 'To the River'
> *Report from the Besieged City and Other Poems*

Through all his years as boatman, fisherman,
he'd answered to the flood
and ebb of tides,
lived subject to the fluent gravities
of moon and sun on water,
day and night through every season,
every turning of his life.

On this day, of all tides
on which he'd ever waited,
this floodtide comes right
on time to serve his going,
one mild day in mid-October
when Mass and prayers were done
in the chapel of St Molleran
and a throng stood gathered on the New Bridge
and by the slipway of Tobar na gCrann,

the priest Tom Flynn
sprinkling holy water on the coffin,
the boat and boatmen ready
on the swell.

The likes of this has not been seen before
in living memory of this river town —
this day on which Willmo Callaghan's

two sons, Ralph and William,
take their father five miles up by water,
the coffin draped in the flag
of his hurling club,
to a resting place beside the river
in the ancient ground of Baile an Teampaill
where a fresh grave lies open to the sun.

A hush falls as the boatmen with their burden
move slowly out midstream to turn
upriver at full tide. A whole town breathes
together, drawn into deep ritual and flow
of things as old as river settlement,
with all that's gone of it or still to come.

People, some in tears,
on quaysides and two bridges,
lift their hands to wave,
applaud or call a greeting,

then bless themselves
as the boat goes by,
as if they know
that something of themselves
is going too.

So these two sons and their dead father
move on to keep a steady course
over the town weir deep in swell of water,
over Friars' Rock submerged, Cora na mBráthar,
the fishing weir by Deerpark at the tide-head,
then press on up against the strength and rush
and slap of Ballinderry current at the bow.

Well he knew this water,
with every submerged stone and mark and drift,
salmon pool or snag or place of drowning —
all that history he held
in deep mist and flow of memory
of men and times and river,
shaped by changeless ways
of flowing water,
moon and sun.

>Now as he's taken up
>against the current
>all he knew in life
>flows off behind.

At Cor' Uí Néill in the Gap of Ballinderry
I point the lens and see in focus
tears on the boatmen's faces
as they come on and breast the current

where others waiting on the riverbank
call out greeting and blessing
as men and women do all along the towpath
beside the sister river in the sun.

On they press upriver
through deep pools
and skirting gravelled shallows,
by Poll Saillí
and Poll a' Bhradáin,
past Dovehill until they reach

the gathering of people
waiting in fields

by the riverside and graveyard
at Churchtown.

With care and ceremony
the coffin's landed,
shouldered in

to the resting place
that he himself has chosen
for the sound of river music
by his side.

When it's over
people seem distracted,
subdued by the clarity
of a story that is

simple
and profound
as flowing
water

telling
in this valley
all that passes
and abides.

PART TWO

Tidings

Helen at the wedding

The universe is made up of stories, not atoms.
　　　　　　　　　　　　— Muriel Rukeyser

Interview on Main Street

So what kind of things do you write about?

Here's one for starters coming down Main Street
though by the time he gets here you'll be gone.
From top of Bridge Street to Barrack Lane and back
is a five-minute stroll for any upright man.
For him it's a slow-motion marathon.

He's learned to stay the course until two o'clock,
and pace himself by window sills and shops —
if you lived here you'd not need to be briefed
on how a vigorous, astute, hard-swearing man
could gear down to such t'ai chi posturing.

How slow is slow before being in a state
of *stopped*? Is this what Einstein was on
about, the gist to the effect that stopped
is just another state of going on?
(Such issues were aired near Slievenamon

one Field Day as the prize was being passed
to the winner of the Slow Bicycle Race
when suddenly up popped another man
claiming he'd just crossed the line, unflagged.
I'm last, he said, and that means that I'm first.)

So far the issue has been one of pace
and we have overlooked our old friend, pain.
There's little here that's worth your while to tape:
try asking two-stick man how things are —
he'll peer at you and answer, *Not too bad.*

Instead you could decide that it's a wrap
and head off to link up with the N7
before he's reached the sill of AllStar Travel.

You could evade rush hour, be home by the time
two-stick man is back at starting point.

Stormy Weather, 1938

i.m. my parents, George and Dora Coady

On their Killarney honeymoon they found
themselves with time and money just run out.
Far off and deep downstream she would tell of
that evening in the bar of Scott's Hotel,
counting small change to make the train fare home
until she walked to the piano and played the intro
to the Harold Arlen song, 'Stormy Weather'
his party piece in those first years together.

Go on! some drinkers called, *go on!* And so
by the night's end the place was full of song,
his hat a well of silver and the proprietor
proposing they stay on, with a retainer.
That given time was never quite undone
by all the weather of the years to come.

A Winter's Night, a Gershwin Song

He'd set out to locate and photograph a holy well but went astray on unmarked roads deep in lush greenery. Go on to meet a sign, he thought, until he found himself entering a small town where something vaguely tugged from his deep memory. He parked the car in the square and then in a sudden rush recalled one winter's night a world ago.

Here's where he'd played at his first dance. The first of all his nights and times as a musician, the recollection fused with a particular song, remembered even to its key of E flat. He was going on seventeen, a learner on trombone, making a nervous debut with his uncle Peter's band. *Orchestra* rather: the musicians wore tuxedos and could read music scores. Two saxophones, trumpet, piano, bass and drums. And, on that night, tentative trombone as well. His initiation among elders, all of them now gone.

Standing in sunshine in that small town again he remembered an archway and a tunnel-like entrance to a spacious dance hall and stage, with a supper room off to the side. Coloured lights and Christmas decorations. It was St Stephen's night. Tea, cooked ham, tomatoes, cream buns and cake and sherry trifle. Music and warm bodies weaving, touching, holding. Perfumed women, sleek-headed men. All subsumed within a winter past.

Here and now, an old-timer sitting in the sunshine on a window sill. Cross over and enquire.

You must mean the Arch, the man said. That was in my hair-oil days for sure. The Arch Ballroom. And cinema that was. Across the square behind you.

A man is summoned from the bookie's. Hugger-mugger about keys. And then he's led to a bricked-in archway between shops. A door set into it is unlocked. Under that arch he steps again as once before, into a long roofed-over passageway like a cave. And there, through swing doors at the end, the hall itself, now a community centre, but essentially unchanged.

Lights flicker on in its windowless and haunted space of memory. Spacious; silent; eloquent. Sound of his own breathing. How mysteriously can chance resolve between intent and outcome. Setting out to find a well, unmarked summer roads return him to this space one winter's night long past.

Look towards the darkened stage.

There they are, who are no more. His mother Dora, still with her good looks, sitting side-stage at the piano. The saxes up front, his uncle Peter standing at the single microphone to sing 'The Way You Look Tonight'. The brass behind, with bass and drums. That shy teenager seated at a music stand, in a badly fitting dress suit, jacket borrowed by his mother from one source, trousers from another. New white shirt and black bow tie for his debut, from Bourke's Drapery, Main St, Est 1806.

Put it down in the book until I settle after Christmas, she said to Hughie Ryan. We have a dance to play for on St Stephen's night.

The trumpet player beside him there, Joe Carroll, who would be friend and mentor to his coming out. Heart of kindness and innocent excitability. Sometimes his embouchure might act up, or his hernia erupt if he overstretched on a high note. Tales of circus bands, brass bands, dance bands, pit orchestras.

Deep into that distant night Joe will lead through the first chorus of 'Love Walked In', then take the trumpet from his lips, lean quickly towards him and above the music shout *Take it!* No time for nerves or backing off. With the next downbeat he's thrust into the lead on slide trombone; breath and lips and pulse of Gershwin song —

Love walked right in and drove the shadows away,
Love walked right in and brought my sunniest day,
One magic moment and my heart seemed to know
That love said hello, though not a word was spoken . . .

One winter's night of going on seventeen. Upstream were all things still to come that would in time be gone. While Joe sat back, the trumpet in his lap, and smiled to hear and see a youngster coming on.

Breast Stroke

Oh, I knew him all right.

The two of us
shared the one desk
below in The Green School,
and summer days
in the river
at the Friars' Rock,

doing the breast stroke
underwater,
eyes wide open,
making mad faces
to get one another to laugh.

Whoever could stay down
longest was the winner.

We used to hunt rabbits
and pick blackberries together,
and catch trout in The Glen
or head off out to Cregg
to gather mushrooms or to rob
Pearl Beary's orchard in September —

I can see her now
like a ghost appearing
at the back of the ramshackle house,
hardly bothering to chase us off,
maybe for want of company
after she came down in the world.

I knew him as boy and then man
all the years that we worked
and drank hard

on the buildings in England.
The two of us steamed up
at the tail end of the night
in Highbury, belting it out

I'm sittin' in a honky in Chicago
with a broken heart
and a woman on my mind.

But the years push on.
The years push on.

The first time he tried it
he botched the job
but he was never a man
to give up or give in
so the second time around
there was no mistake
and he done away with himself.

It was the last job ever he done,
God rest his soul.

Isn't History Great?

Another quiet night in Ellen's. Five souls in their bodies, as follows:

Ellen herself behind the counter, nursing the hip that she hurt. Everything under her wing of the four score years she has known. Serving occasional orders. Drawing and filling for others to empty. Making out change. Listening and dreaming. Chatting and laughing. Reading the court reports in *The Nationalist*. 'He must be a bad egg. And thinkin' he could get away with it.' Patting the scented waves of the perm she got today. Remembering all she remembers. Forgetting whatever she must.

And Bridget, on her own, still mourning her husband. Under the weather this night, rambling and tracing, over and over. Telling herself and the world. Her grandmother taking care of her after her mother died. The time she was sent to bed on a fine summer's evening for raiding the sugar bowl. 'Oh, she was strict all right. But wouldn't let anyone else raise a finger. She was the one that minded me when there was no one to mind me. I'm only a blow-in here from the County Kilkenny since I was sixteen years of age. And I still back the black and amber, though me sons are all Tipp. I lights candles for me grandmother. And I says prayers to her. Isn't history great all the same?'

And two men who meet there each week. Old friends. In the usual corner. Talking of hurling and Hara Cleary who could go through a brick wall. But met with his match in the end. Went to the States in the '50s. His two knees smashed playing mid-field with the New York Gaels against New Jersey's Erin's Own. All the hurlers steamed-up before the game started. That was the training for Gaelic matches those days in America. Tumblers of whiskey all round before the ball was thrown in.

The fifth of the five on this night is the first to head home. Gerry who works for the Council. On the job at eight tomorrow morning, even though it's a Saturday. A grave to be dug for Blackie Maguire. Lying above in the chapel tonight, before he goes down beside the mother and father on Sunday.

The job that has to be done when it has to be done. As it was in the beginning, and as long as this town is standing. The mouth of the earth that has to be opened by someone. Hail, rain or snow, hell or high water, no choice of good or bad day in the matter. Room must be made in the ground. Until the man doing the digging is down in over his head, sweating and swearing under his breath. For Blackie this time, God rest him. A handy half-back when he played with the Swans.

'I'm off,' says Gerry.

'Don't forget your shovel,' one of the men jokes. For Blackie who used to drive the bread van for Galvin's bakery around the town and out the country. Warm batches of loaves fresh out of the oven each morning.

The Inside-out Beckett Umbrella

1

What'll you have to drink?
I got good news today.
The doctor gave me
the all-clear.
Said the heart is sound —
absolutely A1 —
as long as I'm
going downhill.

2

Peg Power the actress
bumping into old Dan Callaghan
the blind fisherman

in the middle of the old bridge
that spans the tiding river
between Carrick Mór and Carrick Beg.

Are you all right, Dan?

I'm grand,
only I don't know
which way I'm facing
or whether
I'm coming
or going.

3

Any luck with the horses?

Loads of luck.
But the wrong kind.

4

Rucksie Ryan
one Monday morning
wheeling his bicycle
out of the cemetery,
a wooden cross
tied to the crossbar,
strong evidence of wet clay
on the base
of the shaft.

No doubt you're wondering.

You could say that.

I'm taking it home
for servicing. They're giving
showers for later on.

5

They tried to tell us we're too young,
Too young to really be in love.
Always his party piece,
even in Sunnyside,
with the head gone on him.

6

She never believes
what I say
but we get on great because
I never tell her the truth
anyway.

7

Three married men
in the same street
in love with me
at the one time.

What did I do?
I wouldn't give tuppence
for any of them.
Billy was my only one

and he
dropped dead on me
one day
at the head of New Street.

I never
got over him
and never
will.

The curse of God
on him
for leaving me down
the way he did.

O Wonderful World of Ironmongery

That Main Street ironmonger
gone crazy for the girl
who takes the bets
skips out of the bookie's
after plunging all again —
then dances, yes, dances

across the street
to his emporium, intoning
'Wonderful, Wonderful Day'
from *Seven Brides for Seven Brothers*
for all who have ears to hear
this forever breaking news

that the world
is still so tenderly
and savagely enraptured
by the holy ghost of lust
that a slip of a girl
(as ever thus in days

of yore or yet to come)
a mere slip
of a girl can still
organically inflame even
a Main Street ironmonger
so as to leave him baritoning

to hammers, saws and chisels,
chains and spirit levels,
locks and six-inch nails —

Beautiful,   glorious,   heavenly,   marvellous,
Wonderful, wonderful, wonderful, wonderful,
Wonderful, wonderful day!

The Mysteries

I

Two women, settled in their ways,
living on the south side of the river.

Every August after hairdos
at Madeline's Salon

they head off by bus on pilgrimage
to Our Lady's Island in south Wexford

where such as they have gone
at harvest time through thick and thin

since Rudolph de Lamporte of that place
was killed on the Crusades.

One of the two is fat, bad on the legs,
the other fine-boned, skinny, sallow —

not a pick on her to feed a maggot
we say, and of the other

it's a wonder she can make it
up the stairs to bed —

as though we need to highlight
and confirm the common

imperfection of the world
that we've been given.

2

In her time the fat woman married,
bore children, buried one;

her soufflés and apple tarts
won prizes at the Barony Meeting.

The other lives alone
and gets on well with solitude;

when she has time to kill
she knits to complex patterns

and is prepared to sit up with the dying,
or lay out a corpse when needed.

Each has known joy and sorrow.
They travel by whatever

light they can envision
and are not blind

to what may darkly
stir in any garden.

3

On Sunday morning each prepares
and dresses in her best,

attending to the ordinary
hunger for the beautiful.

Come hell or high water
they show up in time for Mass,

are usually in place before the priest
who sometimes sleeps it out

following sick calls in the night
or card games with the undertaker.

After *Lord, I am not worthy*
the thin woman and the fat

drink from the chalice and receive
the Host, then each lifts a ciborium

and takes her stance at her habitual place
to share out Communion with the faithful

who come in slow procession and seem
not to be paying much attention

other than to eye
the Nigerian altar girls

and mutter unconsidered
prayers across the pews.

If hymns are sung before or after
the thin woman's in her element,

soaring with a lush vibrato
adopted since she starred as Margot

in *The Desert Song*, live at Marian Hall
when she was young and lusted after.

4

On occasions when the priest's off to a funeral,
or at the greyhound track,

or visiting his mother, the women
fill the gap to lead the Rosary.

The fat prefers the Joyful Mysteries
while the thin goes for the Glorious.

Of the Joyful five the fat one's favourite is
The Finding of the Child Jesus in the Temple

while the thin woman of the Glorious loves best
The Assumption of Our Lady into Heaven.

Both leave the Sorrowful Mysteries
to the priest, and haven't yet

looked into five additional epiphanies
called Mysteries of Light

proposed by Pope John Paul as he
grew closer to the ground he often kissed,

bending day by day under
the cross of his slow dying.

5

Now and then the women find some reason
to be cool with one another

or subtly show up one another's failings.
When hasty words are said

they later make it up, exchanging
tarts and knitting, neither knowing

what the other may be thinking
in her heart of hearts.

And so they incarnate
the nights and days —

two women, settled in their ways,
living on the south side of the river,

dealing with the constant
imperfection of the world,

showing how things are,
and how things hold together.

Asking for Water

What I heard happened was this. The small family had set up a camp down in Ballylynch just before dark. The man had gone in search of dry sticks or anything he could forage from the ditches to light the fire. And the woman went off up towards the little houses. She had a child in her shawl, a little girl of two called Mary like herself, and a small boy, four years old, trailing behind.

The night was coming on stormy and wet. Those little houses at the foot of the hill just up from the river, none of them had running water at the time. But there was a public tap nearby, at the side of the road, and everyone used it.

The traveller woman didn't know that, and it was dark already. She knocked on the door of one of the houses and when the man of the house came out she reached out a gallon can and asked for some water to boil the tea. Give us a sup of water, sir, and you'll have luck for it, I imagine her saying. The man looked at the woman with the child in her shawl, and the small boy behind. His wife was standing behind him and later backed up what he said. *The witness stated that he directed the woman to where the tap was located* was what was printed in the paper.

It all comes down to what exact words were said on that night. Whenever it came up afterwards he always insisted that what he said to the woman was *The water is over there*, pointing towards the tap, and that the traveller woman turned around and went off into the dark where he had pointed. Another thing she didn't know was that it was also the way to the open river close beside them, and there was a big spring tide that night, full in up to the lip of the bank, with wind and rain behind it.

Later on someone found the small boy, drenched to the skin, wandering in the dark on his own on the road, crying and calling for his Mammy. He was brought to the barracks, but the guards could make no sense of what the child was saying, and they put him into the hospital overnight. The travelling man had gone looking for his wife during the night, but he didn't want to go near the guards.

And next morning the terrible sight appeared. The tide was gone out and there, in the streaming mud close to the river-bank, the drowned woman, with the little girl still wrapped in her shawl. The two Marys.

A cloud of shock and grief came down on the town. Then some kind of guilt. And then some need to blame, with hints and mutterings against the man who directed the woman to the water. It was twisted by those that way inclined, maybe to make themselves feel better. Telling it as the poor woman coming with her children to the door on a bad night. Asking for a drink of water, and being turned away, and in the darkness walking straight into the river with her little girl held wrapped to her bosom against the wind and the rain.

The misfortunate man who had directed her to the water was haunted by it for the rest of his days. The boy of four who lost his mother and little sister was taken off up towards Kildare by his father after the burial.

That was sixty-one years ago. Sixty-one years of tides coming in and going out as if nothing had happened. The drowning happened on an Easter Monday. And on that day every year they all come to the grave. The man who was the little boy of four when it happened, with his wife and children and grandchildren and other relations. A whole flock of the clan. And they spend a full day at the grave. They say prayers and eat and drink, and they talk to the dead — to Mary, the little girl of two, and the mother Mary who was only a young woman herself on the night it happened.

They all talk to the two Marys the same as if they were alive there along with them, chatting away, and crying and telling stories and singing and filling them in on all that happened over the past year since they visited. And they tend to the plot. Every inch of it covered in flowers, and little statues and toys and rosary beads and plaques with inscriptions of love.

Passing Predator

Last night it slew him
in a roaring second
on the bog road to Ferbane —

left in its red-eyed wake
all that alert intricacy of nerve
and skin and bone

squashed by the road's edge
where just before oblivion
he'd stood to lift his head

and scent the moonlight
as his kind had done
since long before the first impress

of human foot upon the bog,
and long before
the turn of wheel

or twist of tongue
to name him
broc.

Celtic Tiger, West of Ireland

The Woman of Five Bathrooms

after Mangan

O woman of five bathrooms, to brag is not your way.
You joke about extravagance: what would our grannies say?
Coffee-morning chatter turns to diet and aerobics,
property and liposuction, restaurants and clothes.

Your husband dreams beside you, O woman of five bathrooms,
he plans makeovers of the past to be launched upmarket.
He means to make a killing on some tumbled famine village
(nine cottages, a harbour, views of lake and river).

O woman of five bathrooms, what use all this ablution?
Does money always bring with it a hungering for purity?
He knows where he's going; you wonder what it's for.
Your father lying in the earth. Your mother in a home.

Slide out of the warmth to take a sleeping pill and pee,
then wash your hands, lie down again and pray the dark
   brings ease.
O woman of five bathrooms, the clock blinks through the
   night,
in time this master bedroom will lie open to the sky.

The Open Gate

'We pass through fire and water,' said the black man in an upper room by the West Gate. 'Through water and through fire, my friend. Here you are welcome. And the lady also, though our service is almost finished for today.'

In this third-floor room of a high house full of silenced story.

'Thank you,' he says to the preacher. 'As we were passing home from church we heard singing, too early in the day to be from Nora's bar next door. It drew us on into the lane, then up the stairs. To see what was the story here.'

Once upon a Sunday in September, passing home by the West Gate.

'The story, it is this,' the black man says. 'The holy spirit is the oil. The oil of the morning. And each one of us a lamp. That is the story. The lamp, it must be ready and be worthy.'

And while he speaks resplendent women out of Africa sing praise and soothe their babies in this sunlit upper room. Sing out without restraint in this high house which looks down on the street that dips down to the river that forever seems to leave.

Here where Darby Rourke the dancing master once threw scandalous soirées. *Pléaráca na Ruairceach*. Cardplay. Assignation. Beakers filled. Before last harpers gathered in Belfast.

They sing of light this now and here, the women out of Africa, where revels once were warm in candlelight and shadow. Planxty and quadrille. Bowls of punch. Raised up on a table, the fiddler Kelly and Ó hIffearnáin the piper play 'The Rights of Man'. Until the time of bloodied pikes down-river and public floggings for names of United Men, when Lord Kingsborough had Kelly the fiddler flogged to the bone and then threw salt upon his lacerated back.

'Yes, you are welcome here among us in the Lord's great name. On this day and in this place. Amen.' So says the black man, with alleluias echoed in an upper room by the West Gate.

Behind the preacher, through high windows facing down

to take in Bridge Street, there's Tom Carroll. Trumpet player. Barber. Backlit, on a mission. Leaving his shop again. To slip up to the bookie's and check the odds at Goodwood, Listowel or Longchamps before the off. Then back to heads and hair. Countrymen come in on Sunday mornings. Across the bridge from County Waterford. Talk of weather, harvest, hurling, horses.

'And you too, my lady. Most welcome now, and when we gather here again. We must pass through fire and water but it is the oil of the morning that lights us through the day and through the dark. The oil of each beginning in the spirit, yes. And the lamp that must be ready and be worthy to show light. This is the story of the story. If you wish, do come and join us here again.'

'We thank you,' he says, shaking hands. 'We thank you all.' He almost adds 'in the Lord's name', but hesitates and then refrains.

From its tower outside, the clock above West Gate strikes one. Gatecrashers in their own place, they begin to back away and down the stairs. From eyes of black babies and an outstretched web of hands.

PART THREE

Another River

One day by the Seine I happened to meet . . .

Wharnow are alle her childer, say? In kingdome gone or power to come or gloria be to them farther? Allalivial, allaluvial! Some here, more no more, more again lost alla stranger.

— James Joyce, *Finnegans Wake*

Crash Course in French

At my age let's skip
the Future Perfect
and get by with the Present tense,
some common nouns and greetings,
numbers and directions
and the verb *to be* —

then, for my soul's buoyancy,
slip in a poem or two,
a song or prayer.

But there we go again —
the vista opening up,
the water deepening
whichever way you turn,
whatever raft you cling to.

The Joie de Vivre of Annick and Pierre

for Paul Durcan

Bonjour, Annick et Pierre,
je suis irlandais,
a stranger, chancing by today
out of all the catchment of our lives
and tributary streams of happenstance
it took to carry each of you, and me,
to this, your delta place –

just across the path from where
in Montmartre cemetery
Vaslav Nijinksy is slouched in bronze
over his own grave,
downcast as Petrushka,
immortal puppet yearning always
for a human heart and face.

Nearby, a woman on a bench in April sunshine
turns her head to see
whose photograph I'm taking,
then continues on imperiously
filing her nails, while from another
corner of her eye she oversees
her man, who's within range
and hunting down someone's last earthly
resting place, as I

point the lens to find and photograph
the street snapshot of Annick and Pierre
that someone singled out
in truth and love and grief
to set in stone
between their names and dates.

So there we meet for the first time,
although they can't see me
within their moment's frame. I see

a man and woman, young but not
too young, sure of each other, smiling,
in some time and place, some why and where,
open to whatever's on the way,
hand in hand and stepping out
down a bright street
that leads them on
towards eternity,

flourishing in their free hands
ice creams (*cornets à deux boules*)
they're about to eat.

What are your choice of flavours
on the day,
Annick and Pierre?

Fruit de la passion,
menthe chocolat,
pomme verte
or *jasmin,*

pétale de rose,
vanille
or *caramel,*
framboise or *fraise?*

It lifts my heart to meet you on this day,
Annick and Pierre,
the pair of you

still showing all the living and the dead
how to be human in this world,

hand in hand
and walking with your ice creams,
down some street and round a corner,
radiant and brave,
and just about to taste.

Good Friday

Easter this year falls early, and this
Good Friday cold, with squally showers.
Our *via dolorosa* is the ancient
hill of Geneviève, from Saint-Médard
on up by cobblestones and food stalls
of well-trodden Mouffetard.

This is a working day, as in
the city where the Nazarene
was given a mock trial before the mob,
stripped and beaten, spat upon
and crowned with thorns, then harried
through the streets and up a hill
to be nailed to a cross
and hang there until death came
between two criminals. What were
their names? Their lives and crimes?

The hill of our procession
has known passing feet of men
and women since this settlement
the Romans called *Lutetia* began.

Two thousand years of feet perhaps.
Stalls that hem us in on either side
offer fish and bread and wine.
Some people standing by their wares,
or in doorways, windows,
balconies of upper rooms,
look on and bless themselves
as they see the cross go by,
its wood rough and unvarnished,
borne upfront in their turn
by young women and men
with stops at the set Stations,
rain in our faces, prayer
and chant in Latin and in French.

The way uphill on cobblestone
is slow until we circle Contrescarpe,
then move on via rue Descartes
and rue Clovis to reach the steps
and shelter of Saint-Étienne du Mont,
a sanctuary of lightness, ceremony, grace,
that I have come to know and love.

Inside, the icons on this day
are cloaked in purple.
Ecce lignum crucis sung.
This is also happening now
in the place from which I come
and untold other places
under the sun.

I wait my turn to kiss the cross
held upright by a girl
upon the altar steps; lean forward,
bring my lips to the raw wood

with its deep grain and all it signifies
of suffering and love that all
encounter in the world.

⟿

And so the ultimate humiliation's done.
Christ crucified again,
the torturers once more forgiven
from the bloodied cross of love.

When I emerge there's still
the wind and rain, and overhead
the looming hubris of the Panthéon,
where once stood the ancient church
of Geneviève, with a cross still
high over the dome on this
historic hill above the river

now crowned by the nation's grandiose
temple to the great men chosen
by the state for highest praise
and cells within a stone-cold crypt,
a sanitized Bastille of glorious dead,
safe from sky and wind and rain,
immured under untold tons
of stone no one is ever likely
to roll aside — all this assembly

under the swinging arc and eye
of Foucault's pendulum suspended
from dome to floor, revealing
to the turning world

that the world turns.

Fête de la Musique

Salute the nation that devotes
midsummer day to music of all sorts,
free for all
and in the open air.

I'm blessed to be this day
in the Jardin du Luxembourg
at the only spot that moment
in the wide earthly world
where for midsummer ears
'So What' from *Kind of Blue*
was to be heard

performed outrageously
on insouciant sousaphone and banjo
with interjections improvised

on trumpet (wa-wa mute), tight-rope
trombone, nuanced snare drum
and angular soprano sax in C.

For sure Miles Davis
never saw or heard the like.
Quelle surprise!
Quelle joie!

The Nun in Prison

for Frances Doyle of Carrick Beg and Paris, Soeur Véronique of Les Soeurs de Marie-Joseph et de la Miséricorde.

At the core of the city there's an island in the river,
with bridges to both banks. Like a great ship
at moorings Île de la Cité carries a deep ballast
of history reaching back before the Romans:
even now the bustle and glamour of Paris
flows around and centres on this island, with
the glass-filtered radiance of Sainte-Chapelle,
the Palais de Justice and the great cathedral
of Notre-Dame that tells in stone and paint and glass

more than a thousand years of happening,
of struggle, desecration, worship and intuition
of what lies above us and beyond.
Cheek by jowl with glowing Sainte-Chapelle
there's the Conciergerie where Marie Antoinette
awaited execution, and where there's still
a holding prison —

and that is where I go to meet
with the frail woman from Carrick Beg
who's spent much of her life there.
The last door opens and clangs behind me
after I've stammered my *j'ai rendez-vous
avec Soeur Véronique, s'il vous plaît*
through three checkpoints. She's there
in dim light, smiles and says hello.
We hesitantly half embrace,
as we would not do at home.
After the years her English is laboured.

She takes me to a tiny room,
windowless, for tea and chat
and fresh-baked buns with another sister.
Yes, she gets news of home — friends
or kin send her the little Carrick paper
that she loves. The chaplain's briefed me:
she's been suffering depression and is subject
to a strict Mother Superior. The order's rule
was traditionally hard. Why did some invent
a harsh inhuman Christ of their own making?
But the ruling Mother is away today.

I'm shown the small chapel, dark
and cramped, no glowing stained glass.
We light candles and say a prayer together.

And then I'm led through more locked doors
to open air — their little garden
at this core of the heart of Paris,
a narrow plot with grim buildings
rising high against the sun;
small barred windows all sides
overhead, cells of remand prisoners
and of the nuns. Light reaches
in and down at best in run
to touch the clay, the few flowers
and shrubs of which they're proud.

This woman serving out her days
in a dark place on Île de la Cité
came in poor times, with others
from my town, to join this order.
It must have seemed exotic to
those small-town Irish girls in their time,
going to France, to work for God,
their mission in a secular state
the live-in care of women prisoners.
Face-on they would encounter
darkness of the soul: child killers,
the depraved, the preyed upon,
the lost and hopeless, the doomed innocent,
those broken ones destined to drift
in search of stepping stones across
dark rivers, sometimes lifetimes wide.

This was their work through peace and war,
through wintry times and even hunger.
They say the nuns' dress has an element
of blue to remind prisoners of the heavens overhead,
and that in the past each sister was allowed
to wear a blade with which to cut down quickly

any prisoner found hanging in her cell.
As I spend my few hours with Frances Doyle
I wonder about Socrates and the unexamined life.
He was too wise to discount virtue and humility,
the unseen good done selflessly. Besides, this frail
unhappy woman by my side
does not lead an unexamined life:
she knows where she is, and what
she's given her life to, and why,
even if the world knows not, nor cares.

Now that the cat's away, I joke,
will she come out with me for a stroll?
Yes, she smiles, she's free. On our
way out through the yard we meet
two young prostitutes, all flashy
jewellery and flaunted sexuality.
They've been released after questioning
and fall upon her joyfully —

Chère Véronique! Comment ça va?
They know her for a friend
that they can trust, and politely
shake the hand of this *écrivain irlandais*
from her home town. She wags
a maternal finger in admonishment, saying
she doesn't want to see them back again.
And so they go, laughing with their half-naked
wares, once more out into the world,
the streets and boulevards and pimps.
I wonder what they'll be in forty years.
I know they won't forget Soeur Véronique.

Outside I offer her my arm and we go
strolling by the river, cross Pont Saint-Michel.

Would she like to share some food or drink?
She's happy just to stroll and talk,
past Charlemagne on his high horse
and bristling bodyguards of bronze,
and the great Notre-Dame de Paris
with tourists, pigeons, cameras, sparrows,
devils, angels, saints and kings
fronted by the reference marker: *zéro kilomètre*,
the official navel point of France
from which all distances are measured.
High over all gargoyles, the figure
of Our Lady. We enter the little flower garden
behind the cathedral, find a seat in sunshine.
Spring buds are opening on the trees
and here with the Seine flowing past
she reaches back into her childhood
beside the Suir in Carrick Beg.
She speaks a litany of names, remembrances,
friars and fishermen and cots and floods
and tides; the songs, prayers and poems
she learned by heart at the Presentation,
the skipping games, the griefs she's known.
She says the Hail Mary there aloud
as she remembers it in Irish.
I ask her how the police and prison guards
treat prisoners. 'Sometimes I hear
cries at night. From ones picked up
for questioning. But mostly they are good.'

Within a year I'll learn she's died
while celebrating Patrick's Day. In due course
I'll attend a Month's Mind Mass
in the parish chapel at Carrick Beg
where she was christened —
I still don't know where she's buried.

It's all the one to God, she'd likely say.

But that spring day in Paris the time comes
for me to see her home again
arm in arm to the prison gate
on this river-girded Île de la Cité.

On our way we wait to cross
the roadway on the bridge
where four mounted police, one a woman,
are approaching — handsome, haughty,
high and mighty in the saddle.
Seeing the frail woman on my arm
they rein up, wave us across, doffing
their hats and calling out together —
Bonjour, Soeur Véronique! Bonjour!
She smiles, explaining 'They all know me —
they save the horse-dung for us
to spread on our garden.'

At the prison gate I ask her if
there's anything she'd like me to get
or send to her. She hesitates,
then says half-daringly but shyly
as if exposing sinful weakness —
'*Je voudrais un morceau de* Cleeve's Toffee,
or some strawberry jam.'
The Greeks believed that souls in the underworld
fed on asphodels while they awaited
passage to Elysium.

A Litany for Monsieur Sax

Adolphe Sax, 1814-1894, inventor of the saxophone

Here where you're lying tacet in Montmartre
I stumble on a written message for you, Monsieur Sax —
someone, this side of the dark, proffering thanks,

as I do, for that odd horn you fashioned to release
the unsung voice of brassy reed, or reedy
brass, and for its working parts — the reed,

the ligature, the mouthpiece and the crook, the body
and the bell, the holes, the keys and springs and pads —
and then, in time, out of the melting pot,

those jazzmen you could not have imagined
who blew the horn to life according to their lights
and darks, lips and lungs and souls and fingers,

the place and time, the sidemen and the rhythm,
tangle of circumstance and weather of the heart,
the lines and spaces and the taking off —
> *Play for us*
> *Oh play that thing.*

Yes, Monsieur Sax, I add my breath to thank you
who found yourself twice bankrupt and could never
have foreseen all you'd help make happen

since you were gone before it could begin —
Coleman Hawkins comprehensively caressing
'Body and Soul', or Coltrane one December afternoon

sounding in New Jersey *A Love Supreme*. I hear too
Paul Gonsalves spread full wing at Newport
or Johnny Hodges at the Olympia in Paris make sweet

baroque ballet of 'On the Sunny Side of the Street' —
or Harry Carney, rawhide romantic, have his way
with 'Sophisticated Lady' through all those years

as deep stoker of the sax frontline, letting
all hell break loose in league with the Duke's men —
such extemporizing joy, such carnal utterance —

> *Play for us*
> *Oh play that thing.*

Pity you couldn't have been there, Monsieur, to hear
(perhaps you heard?) all that jubilant menagerie blow on,
give tongue and sing, each one, his given song —

> Lester Young,
> Ben Webster,
> Charlie Parker
>
> *Play for us*
>
> Coleman Hawkins,
> Johnny Hodges
>
> *Play for us*

Stan Getz
and Paul Gonsalves

Play for us

Sonny Rollins,
John Coltrane
and Harry Carney

Play for us

now and at the hour of exaltation
of emptiness and utter absolution

now and at the hour of all serenity
of innermost and outermost extremity —

Play for us
Oh play for us
Oh play that thing.

The Muse in Passing

after Miss. Tic graffito at rue de l'Arbalète

Rules of engagement
not disclosed
on the street
of the crossbow.

Crann Sráide / Street Tree

after 'L'arbre de la rue Descartes' by Yves Bonnefoy

A thaistealaí, féach an crann seo,
seans go gcuideodh sé led' chás

fiú má tá sé salach, gonta,
tá'n dúlra ann, 's an spéir iomlán,

éin ag lonnadh, sioscadh rúnda,
scala gréine in éadan báis —

a fhaidh nó 'fhile, mór an t-ádh ort
crann sráide bheith agat mar scáth,

comharsa theann is tú ag saothrú,
tearmann in aghaidh duibheagáin.

⌣

Passerby, look on this tree,
it could be for you a guide,

though it may be marked or sullied
it embraces earth and sky,

birds alight there, secrets rustle,
death is held up to the light —

lucky you, scholar or poet,
with a street tree nearby,

such a neighbour may sustain you,
holding out against the void.

⌣

No tree now stands
in rue Descartes,

except for the one growing
in the poem of Yves Bonnefoy —

his words told in a mural
with heraldic blue

of Pierre Alechinsky's image
under rain and sun.

Should you pass that way
lift up your eyes,

take time out to grow
between the street and sky.

Mozart and the Kiss of Time

Once more the imperishable
Great Mass in C Minor
after April twilight
gathers in the living with the dead
in L'Église Saint-Eustache,

    citadel of sacred air
    stained glass and stone
    long since become
    a resonating instrument
    not just of sound
    and worship beyond measure
    but also of time —

        First Communion of The Sun King
        baptism and marriage of Molière
        funeral rites for Anne of Austria
        and for Anna, Mozart's mother,
        rampaging mobs during the Terror —

and now this space and time
for a bare-shouldered woman
standing in a beam of light
with woodwind, strings and choir
in shimmering communion.

Tommy O'Brien of Clonmel was right
It's hard to beat the soar of a good soprano

and that swoop may be
upwards or down —

on the solo 'Christe'
of the dark opening *Kyrie*
she drops to sustain a chested

B flat below the stave,
then without a break for air
goes on down to hold a full and tender
abdominal A flat,

the earth suddenly opening
to disclose
a hidden valley, glimpsed

just before a masterful
winged leap
and glittering ascent
to high crescendo
of impassioned
cry to Christ
for mercy

in notes Mozart first penned
for his belovèd Constanze.

The woman bathed now in light
fills the entire space with sound
out of her soul and body,
for this is both ethereal and earthly.
As she takes flight,
there, off to the side
in a half-dark aisle,

       a man and woman standing,
       enfolding one another,
       and taking their time —

that mystery of which the dead alone
have no end,
while the living must go on

with whatever share
they're given —

    taking their time
    in their sustained embrace,
    in their deep kiss

against music perfected
though unfinished, late
in a short life that would
become immortal.

He's here now,
and blessing
the couple in their loving,
longing perhaps to be
again among the mortals
and their singing.

The Hunger

The stone's in the midst of all.
　　　　　　— W B Yeats, 'Easter 1916'

Near where the Romans
stretched and loitered at their baths
every day a man squats

in the centre of the sidewalk
unmoving in the flow
of passing feet,

eyes down, tin cup,
cardboard inscribed
J'ai faim.

Streams of passersby divide,
going both ways
at either side,

while others in their thousands
rush darkly on
deep underground

trusting that they know
where they've come from,
where they're headed to.

Children of Montparnasse

A footnote to the cemetery plan

*Tatiana Rachevskaia, who
rests in Montparnasse*

The great and famous are
the mainstay of *Le Plan du Cimetière*
they'll give you at the gate —
since some high-profile residents
belong to all this world
as well as to the next

and are never short of callers
leaving flowers, gifts or notes
personally dropped off
at this last-known address of, say,
Beckett, Sartre, Baudelaire.

On a visitation round one day
I peered through the metal grill
over one grave and met the beady eye
of a pigeon on her nest

reminding me I'd heard of a man
who lived on this demesne within
an accommodating tomb
and got up every morning
just like the rest of us —
except on days the weather looked
less than hospitable.

That day just as I'd left the pigeon
in the violated gloom, obsessively
intent on her egg,
I had a frustrated text from Ireland:
the sink was blocked up once again
and she was inclined to lose
all faith in plumbers.

This, we must admit, is how
most of life goes on
this side of the quotidian divide
between us and Parnassus.

⤳

After you have wandered up and down
with map in hand
under the solicitude
of Horace Daillion's
'Angel of Eternal Sleep'
and found or failed to find the famous
you should sit down
and close your eyes
to brood upon your egg

and try to restore the lost time
when the many thousands lying
prone in dense divisions here
were all in their time still little
children, over ground, and playing —

picture it: live children playing —
as children do, always
and everywhere,
every single one,

even those yet to be
among the famous
or infamous.

Then imagine, if you can, when
this ground was woodland, pasture,
not quite an Eden garden

but not a single tear yet shed
into its earth,
or wreath laid down,
or delving done

though some there were already
on chance paths to this
still virgin ground
where in time they'd prove
to have been bedded.

But then why stop at recalling
them as children ready-made?
Let's have each life, each river,
turn around and flow
upstream to its beginning,
that impassioned moment
when each life here began,
each with its own incarnating *pas de deux* —
most probably performed in bed,

or as the case may be/have been
in instances beyond our ken
(how we'd love to know)
when procreation happened
in intimate association with

barns, boats, ships, rivers,
lakes and seas, sofas, tables, floors
and firesides, desk-tops, prisons, corridors,
hospitals, hotels, railway embankments, carriages and carts,
brothels, churches, graveyards, battlefields, haystacks,
monasteries, motor cars, shops, theatres, parks,
swamps, sand dunes and tents, rafts, meadows,
deserts, forests, hills, mountain slopes

or even mountain tops
such as that fabled one
of glorious Apollo.

In league with any one of these
the quintessential ballet of begetting
may be staged —
for there's no couch or setting
that may not be enlisted in
that old blind conspiracy between
the phallus and the womb.

⤳

And thus the peopling
of this earthly or unearthly
estate began and carried on
once the blood, sweat and pain,
screams and opening cries
of birth in every instance here
had been accomplished
in accordance with some master
plan that's still a mystery.

Now having reached this point
with your eyes closed
add in an everlasting note
from all around:
the piping cries and calls
of all those children playing,

such sounds as you may hear
in any street or alleyway,
schoolyard or playground
anywhere —

high voices filtering through trees,
across fields or walls
or from beside a lake or stream
or from a commonage or beach —

in any tongue on earth
that music that you hear
is still the same high-pitched
excited orchestration.

And there as well, in counterpoint,
the mothers of all these,

reassuring, kissing, scolding,
salving cuts and falls,
stings and bruises,
fevers,

and calling children
home,

calling them all in,
each and every
small child here

who will be,
were and are
the famous or forgotten
lined up and laid down
in Montparnasse divisions —

before the night
comes down,
before the storm begins
or sickness comes, or soldiers,

every mother
calling her child
home

before the light is gone,
the lamps are lit,
the windows
shuttered.

*The resting place of Tatiana Rachevskaia,
with Constantin Brancusi's 'The Kiss'*

Sunday Afternoon at Auvers-sur-Oise

La tristesse durera toujours. / The sadness will last forever.
— attributed to Vincent van Gogh on his deathbed

So much that is still as usual
in summer — the village market
chatter in the sun,

the candle flicker in the chapel
where Salomé still accepts
the head of John the Baptist,

the river that seems scarcely to move
or to have moved, the street
with Sunday strollers and their dogs,

the tavern and the narrow stairs
to the tiny attic room
in which he slept those last months

and soon would die, the open air outside
to which he carried
all his gear strapped to his back

to paint the last pictures
in a frenzy — the oils not dry on one
before another was begun.

At the village park a fête:
children doing cartwheels to music,
men and women dancing;

up the hill in unrepentant sun
the graveyard and the grave
where a man sits painting

a Sunday watercolour
of the brothers' headstones,
side by side, with ivy;

outside the graveyard wall
the wheat field almost ripe
and, yes, the crows

and a woman   Japanese   with a white
parasol against the blaze of sky,
the shimmer of the fields.

Van Gogh sculpture at Auvers-sur-Oise
by Ossip Zadkine (1890-1967)

PART FOUR

Traces

To live is to leave traces.
— Walter Benjamin

Beethoven and the Leaves

Listen, listen,
on this day
of All Souls —

a deaf, dead man
refusing to sing dumb,

his unquiet song
flung *appassionato*

over leaves and candles,
the river
and the world.

Between the Beats at The Moorings Bar

Will you chance the waltz?

It isn't a waltz.
But he'll dance a waltz to it anyway,
knowing no better, and she'll chance it

along with him, neither aware of how hard
it would be to do what they're doing
if they knew what it is they are doing

which is dancing together
in irregular three-four time
to a steady four in the bar

while at the same time
facing opposite ways
but towards each other,

not yet glimpsing anything of all
they begin to dance into being
between the beats

including those still unconceived
who in time will stand and weep
over each in turn.

Fionnuala Grieving at Checkout 5

She sometimes forgets
the discount on bacon
that's near its sell-by
or coupons she should offer
for holidays or wine.

Some days
she can't hide
the desolation in her eyes
from those of us
who wait in line.

Dusk at Inishlounaght

She stood unmoving a distance away
with night coming down on the river:
a young woman
among leaning stones
where vague disquiet of early spring
settled with slow gravity.

It chanced somehow that he should be
there at that same time as she,
each careful to seem
unaware of the other.
About them, words of love and grief,
the earth's embrace, its constancy.

Slow Air

What happened him was
he fell for a woman
from up around Leitrim
or somewhere like that —

she was

All
Ireland
Slow
Air
Champion

three years in a row

and she destroyed him
night and day
with her laments.

The Friday Rounds

The whole town knows Friday is my day out, starting off in Carrick Beg. Most times I'd make a quiet start with a pint at The Clinic. If the day isn't too bad along the way I'd pull in to visit the mother and father in the Friary, along with the sister that died of cancer. And I might visit a few more acquaintances there while I'm at it. Then I'd slip out the back gate near where Johnny Ager the flute player is buried and start to work my way down through the town, dropping in to Maggie Dunne's and The Whistler's, before heading back over the bridge to Carrick Mór.

That's where I'd have a bite to eat and then it's mostly meeting friends along the way till I get home, usually in good order at the tail end of the night after a nightcap in The Bell and Salmon or The Jockey Club.

An odd Friday I might happen to run into Sonny Flanagan. We're blood brothers since our First Communion. He might only be on his way to the bookie's or down to Tom Carroll in Bridge Street for a haircut but if the two of us happen to run into one another we could end up on the tear in The Shebeen at the corner of Castle Street. A man was shot dead there one time back in the Troubles.

Sonny gets a bit boisterous once he hits the shorts. I'm an all-round man, he shouts, landing the fist on the counter. I can fuck, fight and play the melodeon. Several times it happened that the squad car had to throw us a lifeline in the small hours at the West Gate and pilot us home to our own front doors, fair play to the sergeant.

Sonny is a hoor to keep calling for whiskey and boasting about all the eels and trout we caught in our time and the great cards we played in Jimmy Crowley's in our hair-oil days. Hardly a word to throw to a dog when he's on the dry, but a different story when he's drinking and constantly breaking into song. Help me make it through the night, over and over and driving the whole place cracked. Then calling on me to give, Are you warm are you real Mona Lisa.

When he's on it he's on it, but harmless at the back of it all. Didn't we happen to meet up today? he shouts. Yesterday is dead and gone, and tomorrow's out of sight. Shouting across the bar to Natasha before we call it a night. Natasha! Take the ribbon from your hair. Jameson twelve year old, and skip that stuff that sank the *Titanic*. Shake it loose and let it fall. Lay it soft against my skin. Like them feckin' shadows on the hoorin' wall.

The Electric

The man they call Far Distant
plays the box
and comes from the butt
of the mountain.
A brother lives there
along with him
but hasn't been seen
since he was let out of St Declan's.

He never got in the electric.

Imagine nights out there —
Uisce Soluis in spate
roaring and sluicing down
above them in wild weather.
The house is in an awful state,
Nurse Farrell says — two men
and a dog, with no woman
to house-train them.

He never got in the electric.

Calm nights you might hear music
in the dark, coming and going
between the blind hollows
under Coumshinaun.
From way off you'd know
it could only be Far Distant
herding bits of tunes
whose names have been forgotten.

He never got in the electric.

Sunday nights he's paid to play.
He sits in the pub corner,

looking through the wall,
drawing air in with open arms,
then squeezing out raw sounds
that bring whoops from the dancers.
The untamed beat
is earthed through their feet.

He never got in the electric.

Listen while I tell you . . .

from the traditional text 'Céad glóire leis an Athair'
as sung by Cór Chúil Aodha with Peadar Ó Riada

Listen while I tell you
of one that death has taken,
it is Seán Ó Duibhir a' Ghleanna
for all of his fame.

His hounds and all his horses
are gone down, like their master,
and no one knows the dwelling
of the soul from his breast.

For Death is a sly trickster
who silently comes stealing
into every harbour
as sure as the tide.

So since we all must answer
let God's angels guard us
for they will bear our souls up
to the home of the saints.

Then all glory to the Father
whose name the whole world praises,
all powerful in Heaven
and over all men.

He made and clothed angels
in radiance and beauty
devoid of imperfection,
bright as the sun.

The clouds and skies he gave us
and moonlight to guide us,

with stars forever shining
by night overhead.

He filled each stream and river
with their flowing bounty
and the wide and sounding ocean
made teeming with fish.

With trees he filled the woodlands
lofty in their blooming,
and birds upon the branches
to praise him in song.

Not least of all, the bees,
to them he gave a living
and taught them all the wisdom
they needed to learn —

for when the sun is shining
they gather up the honey
to store until it's needed
when winter comes in.

Sheela na Gig

Not a sinner in the Hen and Chickens except your woman herself, and the place half in darkness.

She had an old wind-up gramophone creaking away on the bar and she was out on the floor on her own, waltzing around with a broom. 'Gentlemen,' she said, panting a bit but not stopping, 'I'll be with you in a minute. "Roses from the South." You can't beat Vienna. City of dreams.' Turning her head and talking to us over her shoulder as she swayed and circled around, leaving a wake of perfume.

Jimmy and I looked at one another. She had a long black dress on her, and a pile of old jewellery. Lipstick and rouge in plentiful supply. Death warmed up.

'Oh dear me,' she said, brushing her forehead with the back of her hand when she got behind the bar and took off the old record. 'It could bring on palpitations.'

'You're feeling the heat,' said Jimmy.

'You have to stay on the move,' she said. 'Keep the joints supple and the circulation going. From the heart to the extremities and back. Constantly maintaining bodily temperature in all parts. My ballet teacher had a saying: Horses sweat, men perspire and women glow. Miss Villiers-Stuart. Will I ever forget the harvest dances at the Riding School in Curraghmore? What can I get you, gentlemen?'

I called for a pint of stout and Jimmy called the same.

'Certainly,' she said. 'When you have a thirst on you where would you come except to the fountain? And you're both heartily welcome to the long-established house known as The Hen and Chickens, licensed seven days for wine, beers and spirits, in the townland of Coolnahorna, in the parish of Mothel, in the Barony of Upper Third, in the County of Waterford and the Principality of Déise.'

'On the ball,' said Jimmy. 'And straight into the back of the net for the blue and white. I wasn't sure whether or not we were on course. Or if the natives were friendly.'

'Weren't we great to find our way?' I said. 'Especially on

these dark nights, and not a map or a signpost in sight.'

'A case of here goes helter-skelter and see where you end up,' said Jimmy. 'I remember the Riding School dances. And the sport and play in The Laurels beside it. Great nights gone by when we were full of jizz. But we're still above ground, all the same.'

'That's a plus,' she said, starting to pull the two pints. 'Maybe we met up there sometime. At the Riding School dances. Maybe our paths happened to cross on one of those nights gone by. How could you ever remember the names or faces of all the people you had a whirl with over the years?'

High up on the shelves behind her was a glass case with a mildewed trophy and a faded picture of a greyhound, lit up like a holy shrine. While the pints were settling she put on another scratchy old record. 'Anything fresh from Carrick?' she asked, letting us know that she had the two of us sized up.

'Nothing strange,' I said.

'Nothing strange or startling around here either. No recent murders or major eruptions. Nothing shocking or scandalous. No lightning strikes or miraculous apparitions to report. No sign of anyone coming back to tell us what to expect. Beyond the veil, I mean. No news at all from that direction in this month of the Holy Souls. Lips all sealed. I suppose that's the story all over?'

'No different in Carrick anyway,' said Jimmy. 'The usual capers over ground. And mum's the word in the boneyard. Not a word of complaint from any of the residents.'

'No one giving anything away,' I added. 'Not a sinner spilling the beans.'

'Spilling the beans,' she said. 'Isn't it a queer saying?' She bent over the drinks. 'They'll be ready in a jiffy. A pint of stout must be pulled slowly for best results, as you well know, I'm sure. Can you excuse me for a minute, gentlemen?'

She left the door from the bar open behind her and went up the stairs, sprightly enough. Then we could hear her above, humming away, another door opening. The two of us standing there below at the bar, mesmerized, gazing at the two pints settling.

Next thing we could hear the flow starting up, straight over our heads. Like a downpipe gushing into a barrel after the heavens opening. Jimmy whistled through his teeth.

'Amen sweet bucking Jamesestown. I hope you brought a large umbrella.'

'The meeting of the waters,' I said.

'The blue bloody Danube,' said Jimmy. 'With the tide running out. What possessed us to pull in here?'

Our two drinks still settling and untasted. The place half in darkness, a Viennese waltz winding down slower and slower and groaning to a halt. More gurgling, flushing and creaking above.

'Excuse me!' she shouted down the stairs, the voice up to high doh. 'Excuse me! Could either one of you two gentlemen kindly assist in zipping a lady up?'

Exposure

*A photograph is not only an image (as a painting
is an image), an interpretation of the real; it is also
a trace, something directly stencilled off the real,
like a footprint or a death mask.*
— Susan Sontag , *On Photography*

I know each stone and tree
between The Dasher Power's
and Ballinderry current
where I once fished for salmon —

anglers whose paths crossed
would stop
to ask each other
'Did you meet anything?'

Now, when I walk the riverbank
two miles above the town,
I carry lens and shutter.
The catch I meet today

takes me by surprise,
as it too is surprised
in 1/80 of a second
at an aperture of f4.5 —

a shoe for evening wear,
stylish and unblemished,
that some woman left or lost
here at the riverside,

far from the road above
from which she must have come
unless she came by water here,
or left that way.

I look out into the folding
and unfolding sweep of river,
then probe and peer
through undergrowth,

walk upstream and down,
find no clue and come
to pause again over
the woman's shoe

while the river mimes
and mutters on
unceasingly
in its own tongue.

When I turn and head for home
I've a story clear as day,
telling only what's
inside the frame.

The Half-light of History

1 AT A KILLING FIELD
Dún an Óir, Smerwick Harbour, County Kerry

The word this July day
from Gort a' Ghearradh,
Gort na gCeann,
is just how ordinary
everything's become
across the years,
the centuries —

the flowers and summer
grasses in their place,
the ambient soundscape
of lark-song, reed-whisper,

and the distant
cries
of children
from the shoreline.

2 SCHOOL TOUR, KILMAINHAM JAIL

These kids could scarce imagine
a lost dawn chorus greening on the air
above the Stonebreakers' Yard,

the swell of birdsong shattered
by an imperious voice
commanding thunder.

Yet the children's presence in the yard
in itself is part of aftermath and story,
while far removed from Maytime

fusillade or instant aftershock
that triggered prayer and rage
and terror in the cells

against the muffled orders
for the tidying away
and brisk disposal of the parts

before the sluicing of the stones
in blushing water —
some forgotten

orderly of empire
baptising the beginning
of its end.

PART FIVE

All Waters

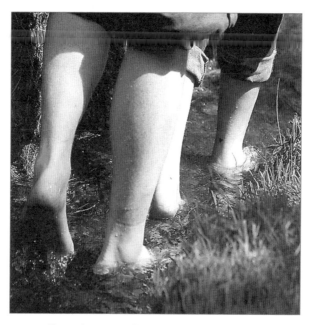

Walking the stream from the blessèd well of Cuan

All waters are one . . .
 — Wendell Berry, 'The Hill'

Three Down

i.m. John Lovett, Tommy Finucane, Brian O'Keeffe

We began with simple hearts,
but suddenly one friend is cancelled out
and the long subtraction starts.
    — Michael Hartnett, 'The Old Catechism'

Brian, when I learn you're gone I'm once again
back there where we were all invincible.
Now three of four are down, one left to speak.
I dial Ireland and hear your wife weep
across the ocean and the years. When we
were learning things by heart we never dreamed
that this is what we'd come to know, to top off
Maths and Shakespeare, Latin, Fiannaíocht.

Last day of school the clock struck four and we
proposed to meet each year whatever happened.
But then the water deepened with the days
and now it's down to words across salt waves
until I have to plead, in truth, *There's someone*
knocking on the door and I must go.

        Villanova, Pennsylvania, May 2005

Tender is the Rain

*at the grave of Scott and Zelda Fitzgerald, St Mary's
Church, Rockville, Maryland*

They'd think us voyeurs
at the lip of the grave
if they were here
aside from what's shed of them

and turned to clay
oblivious and inseparable
in this second bed
of their posthumous pairing —

where their child, Scottie, is also
come home in the end,
as once she lay
and was cradled.

But supposing they
could hear or care
then I'd admit I'd be elsewhere
if it hadn't rained today —

truth is, I chanced to be passing
and am drawn by the implicit eloquence
of this kind of closed
and open place —

a timeworn ground
resigned to decay,
but also a place of the heart
and its breaking,

its gravity based
not on death

but on lives
and their mystery.

What I most feel
chancing by on this day
is the nakedness here,
the pain and courage

and rage of the pain
brought down at my feet,
the folly and grace
and flame that they made

of the nights and days,
apart and together,
raising hell,
or in it —

all that they risked, threw away,
and all that they somehow
saved of the thing before
the burnout and the bell.

On this wet day my wife
checks exposure and focus
to disclose to the future a past
where I'm found by a tilting marker

at the head of a limestone slab
with a sodden, dead bouquet
and the carved closing sentence of Gatsby,
weathering, just as it says.

What's left to tell here
today, this side of the grave?

A few birds are singing
and out on the highway

beyond the wet trees
traffic ceaselessly flows.
Otherwise here and now
a hush as of something in waiting

while things break
down
and fall
into absolute

place
in the rain.

Dunville Old Folks' Home

Cape Shore, Newfoundland

Every night when lights are dim
and eyelids down
the sleeping racket rises

among old-timers out of
Branch, Fox Harbour,
St Brides and Angels Cove.

They dream of whales and winters,
of children, rum and storms,
priests and rowing dories,

of drownings and of meadows,
dances and salt fish,
moose and muzzle loaders.

The dead rise up behind
closed eyes and stir
in toothless jaws.

Lost in his second sleep, Bill
Foley and his father navigate
in fog without a compass,

Phil Tobin who's a hundred
splits fish with old Careen
who's buried in The Barrens

and Maggie Brennan plays
with her dead sister by
the brook in *Gleann an Cheo*

named by her great-grandmother
who sailed out from Waterford
long lifetimes ago.

Seldom Come By

Fogo Island, Newfoundland

The old woman sits in a house in Seldom Come By and remembers her mother's death in Bonavista, when she was twelve and her father away at sea, seventy years ago. She is small and brittle, but her back is straight.

In a frail voice she reaches for a thread of memory and begins to stitch a delicate lace of words over her nested hands. One tear slips from behind her glasses. It falls in her sleeve, and into her childhood.

Her grandmother leads her to her mother's room to kiss the intimate face, strangely chill between sheets. Neighbours come. A meal is prepared. Her grandmother hangs out the washing. It is spring and there are icebergs in the bay. In three weeks her father returns from the sea and stands over the grave without speaking.

From an ocean away I recall the thread of the old woman's voice restitching time. Her grandmother is alive again and hanging out clothes and sheets. See the young girl. She lifts her eyes from the moulded earth to look up at her father standing, wordless, in the wind.

Al Careen, Irish Newfoundlander, Cape Shore

Elementary

A place for everything
and everything in its place
said the grandmother
in my head as I

was bailing water
out of the boat
and back
into the river

as though it would
stay there then
or ever.

Water under the Bridge

People who have been away for years come back here expecting everything to be just as they left it. Getting worked up as if they should have been consulted or informed before any change happened. You'd meet them on the bridge, asking about those little houses that used to be there in Gorey Lane or beside the Fair Green. Or enquiring about the whereabouts and well-being of a certain tree, or some boy or girl they courted or were in the same class with in school.

Dead, you say to them.

Only last week. Or last August. Or twenty years ago.

Dead?

Yes, dead and gone.

You can't be serious!

You'd swear they expected no one to die while they were away wherever it was all those years. People still alive in their heads even though they could be long gone by the wayside here. Though when you come to think of it we're living here all the time and we can never get over it either. People being constantly swept away. The oldest story in the book. But we can't really credit it. As though each death was some kind of slip-up that shouldn't have happened.

Imagine how long all this is going on in the world. Back to the caves or to Adam and Eve. Paddy Finn used to say that God must have been very innocent to leave the pair of them unattended there in the garden without a stitch on them. And then when they were expelled on account of blotting their copybook what was the story from that day out only people making other people and then dying off in time to make way for more of the same?

That's the story, as sure and certain as the river flowing under this bridge for the last five hundred years or the tide going out and coming in by night and by day. But still and all, when there's a death we think it must mean a slip-up on someone's part. Some miscalculation that was not in accordance with the master plan, whatever that is. As if someone

screwed up somewhere along the way. You know the way it
goes on —

Did you hear who's dead?

Gone? Ah no. I don't believe it. What happened?

Stopped breathing, that's what. Gave up the ghost. The
machine conked out. Whose fault? The doctor took the eye
off the ball. Or the patient didn't eat the right foods or take
enough exercise. Shouldn't have been smoking or drinking
or going on skites to Tramore Races or Puck Fair or the
coursing in Clonmel. Or shouldn't have been in that place
and time when the truck with bad brakes happened to come
down the hill. Or under that particular tree when the light-
ning picked it out for special attention. Or they shouldn't
have been asking for it by living to be ninety. Or by being
alive at all in the first place.

I remember the night my father died. When I was still living
at home before I got married. He went suddenly. An hour
earlier he was singing a song. And an hour later dead in my
arms. He's gone, my mother said. He's gone. May our Blessèd
Mother and St Joseph take his soul to God. White as a sheet

and shaking with the shock of it as she starts to cry and goes down on her knees beside me with my father still warm in my arms. His heart after packing it in at last. One thing I never forgot. His eyes were open and then, all of a sudden, without a blink of his eyelids something was gone out of them, and that was that. He was gone. Gone from this world. I could see the sudden absence in his eyes.

The priest and the doctor landing in the door then together. In a sweat the two of them, but too late. It was half-one in the morning. We had to get help to lay out the body before rigor mortis would set in. Amazing how soon everything starts to change. With the human body, I mean. Peg Millea, God rest her, got up out of her bed to come and do the job, helped by Seamus McGrath who had only called in to sympathize.

They laid the body out in a pair of my own pyjamas, washed and ironed and ready for me in the hot press. When my mother ironed them earlier that day she little knew what she was doing it for. That's what he was buried in and I often thought of it after, standing by the grave. My pyjamas down there, like a part of myself gone down with my father. And nothing wrong with that.

That night he died I slipped out to the back garden to calm myself down and take a few breaths of air. I looked up at the sky. Clouds moving along with a moon behind them. Everything just normal. Everything in place. I expected something would have changed because of what had just happened. *My father is dead,* I said out loud in the dark. He's in there, dead in the room. He was born one day in this town and lived here all his life except for a couple of years in America when he was twenty. He was my father and now on this night he's gone from this world forever.

I was muttering out loud to myself and the sky and the dark. And then a dog a few doors down heard me and started barking. As normal as that. A dog barking in the dark. No change in the heavens or the earth. You'd be in shock. You know yourself. Like a belt on the back of the head. And then people around the neighbourhood hearing of the sudden death and coming to our door, even in the middle of that night. Shaking your hand or putting their arms around you. Sorry for your trouble. I didn't know how important those words were until then. *Sorry for your trouble.* And I learned more respect and sympathy for other people. Just ordinary people noticing and paying attention. Knowing what was after happening, and coming to you. Taking the trouble. Can I do anything? Do you need anything? He was a decent man. And talented. Never done any harm to anyone.

Whether they mean all of it or not is neither here nor there. You learn we're all in the one boat, along with all our oddities. All heading in the one direction down the river. And others coming on in their time and in that same boat again. That's how it goes, on and on.

People in the beginning must have been puzzled when they saw dead ones for the first time and just waited around for them to wake up again. I used to joke with Joe Walsh the undertaker. A great man for the game of poker and heading off to the Cheltenham spring meeting. Joe, I used to say, you're the man with the harvest that never fails.

They have to die for me to live, he'd say with a grin, raising his big black umbrella to shield himself from the wind and rain on a bad day at the head of a funeral crossing the river.

And now he's gone himself, with a son gone as well, but the others carrying on.

What I'm really getting at is that people never get used to it as a normal fact of life. It's the one thing we all know about and are sure and certain of. Absolutely sure and certain. But there's a part of us that won't really believe it. Or we secretly think that if we can keep the boat watertight for ourselves and the ones we're fond of then it won't come near us.

And then it arrives at your door, choosing its own time. The shock of it taking the legs from under you, along with the grief and loss that goes on and on. And no remedy ever in the world. But still deep down we think it's a mistake and should never have happened. If we had even a glimmer of sense we'd know that only for the constant clear-out there wouldn't be enough breathing space in the world. Think of the great multitude that's dead and gone out of this town over the years.

I love that word since I was a child hearing about the miracles and the parables. The great *multitude*. Just imagine the number like myself and yourself that crossed over this old bridge in one direction or the other over the last five hundred years. Those that there's neither sign nor light of nor name nor mention of anymore. People that were here every minute of every day and night and year of their lives but that we couldn't even dream about or imagine.

How many in all? In this town alone and constantly crossing over this bridge in their time? You couldn't fit them into this valley. Or if you did they'd be elbow to elbow and breathing down one another's necks. Or maybe at one another's throats. Or probably just getting up to all the usual capers, if they could find the room.

Bob Power, riverman, in the days of his failing sight

Many's the salmon went up under that bridge in all the days and nights, and I met my share of them in my time . . .

Easter Vigil, Massachusetts

After long rituals
of fire and water, word and song,
we leave St Malachy's and step
into the dark where snow
in ghostly mounds still holds out
by roadside and Easter fields.

Driving home, she asks
if we'll come with her to visit
Michael on this night.
We find the place
and then the grave
between deep-shadowed groves.

Don't the moon look lonesome?

She shakes her head in disbelief,
then stoops to light a candle
above the frozen ground
and her firstborn,
shot down five years ago
a thousand miles from here.

Three times the lighter fails.
We hold our breath
until fire catches and she can set down
the little flame beside
the stone that tells his name,
his given years.

Don't the moon look lonesome?

The mother stands upright,
draws courage or defiance from the cold.
She speaks of him as infant

and as boy, as youth and man
murdered at random.
She liberates her tears.

Far off to the south
another woman's son
is serving life this Easter night
for the one who's buried here.
Behind us as we leave
a faint light flickers where we've been.

Don't the moon look lonesome
shinin' through the trees?

Never Again

The present
Is too much for the senses,
Too crowding, too confusing,
Too present to imagine.
      — Robert Frost, 'Carpe Diem'

That's where glasses were drained
over the turn of last cards
once on an autumn night
of those unmarked nights,

each one unique to that place
and those women and men
since no night ever
comes round again.

That's where they stood up
in the now of then
after habitual rounds of talk
and cards on that rainy night

that, as it happened,
would happen to be
the last of those nights
when they turned to make

for the homes they'd go to
under stroke of twelve just gone
high over their heads
on the Town Clock bell

still marking time above
onetime West Gate.
See that empty space
where the bar was then

with its rained-on roof and walls
and the door she bolts
behind their tipsy goodnights
dying away on the flow

that empties and fills each place
as now without fail
becomes then
even as then makes

way for another
now such as this now of mine
and this now of yours
ever and always becoming

never again.

Old Flame

O uncoy mistress, flagrant flower of anarchy,
although few love you, let me say I do.
Once more you're fecund in a million places
mocking all the tidiers and trimmers,
the lawn control-freaks and the poison sprayers.

O ageless banner and time bomb of spring
beyond the pale but everywhere within,
O pissabed and laughing tooth of lion,
every year you're back like an old flame
inciting me to rise and come again.

Ballinderry Fruit

*We are all looking for something of extraordinary
importance whose nature we have forgotten . . .*
    — Eugène Ionesco, *Present Past / Past Present*

So we have lived another year
and come again to this riverbank
at harvest time in Ballinderry
to gather wild fruits where
we know we'll find them —
blackberries, crab-apples, damsons,
sloes and elderberries
to be blended and preserved
for our daily bread
through winter mornings.

On this calm evening
peace is palpable.
In a while my wife moves on
from where I idle, my fingers stained
by berries, pricked by brambles. I recall
the salmon I encountered here years past
and lost or landed in all weathers.

She's heard me tell time and again
of the silver twenty-seven pounder
that I took in on rod and line
here at Ballinderry current one March day,
how I strapped it to my back and cycled
home to the town, in triumph,
got my father out of bed
to celebrate in White's of Lough Street.
Now I'm content to leave all salmon
unmolested on their odyssey
from stream to river, then to ocean
and then, in time, back home again.

I sit down as early dusk begins to gather,
look across the river towards
the ruined castle of Millvale. Then suddenly
the running water strangely changes
key. From the corner of my eye
I glimpse the figure of a child above me
on the riverbank, reaching to pick
blackberries and eat.
She half turns and moves
down closer, steps barefoot into shallows,
begins to wash her hands and feet.

Then, as though in some compelling dream,
I envision Mary Brunnock as this child,
born on the heels of famine and now
standing barefoot in the shallows.
She can't see me because I am of the future,
out of a past I know of, one
that for this child of Ballinderry
hasn't yet begun to happen —
her past future that will link
her story with my kin,
with this late September evening,
this moment by the river.

I know that still upstream
of this child in shadow
there's an ocean crossing and a marriage,
a widowed boatman and lost father,
an orphaned boy who'll be abandoned
in Oven Lane beside this river.

In lives and tides to turn
I'll come in time to stand over
her unmarked grave
in Philadelphia where she'll lie,
a mother dead in childbirth,
and be lifetimes forgotten. There,
in New Cathedral Cemetery

knowing what I know
of consequential pain
and wounded hearts
I'll come to pray for her, her sister Margaret,
her dead children by the boatman
that she'll marry —

for the river flowing towards
this shadow child, this woman,
will be one of tears.

Above the boreen I think I hear
a mother's voice faintly calling
Come up, come home, tá'n oíche 'teacht.
The shadow child is gone,
the presequential dream.

My wife returns,
enough fruit gathered.
Twilight thickens as
I tell her why I am distracted,
moved and shaken by compassion
for the lost shade of one born here
lifetimes ago in Ballinderry
who grew and played

with sisters and with brothers,
picked blackberries
and waded in the shallows.

My wife is silent in the fading light.
We take up the fruit we've gathered
and walk home by the darkening stream.

The Great Embrace

Exultation is the going
Of an inland soul to sea,
Past the houses — past the headlands —
Into deep Eternity —
                        — Emily Dickinson

Always and ever
communion of three sisters
Siuir, ocus Eóir, is Berba
finding confluence over and over

at Cumar na dTrí nUisce
in Waterford Harbour
of Vikings and of Irish,
of Flemings and of Normans,

of West Country men
from Devon
and from Dorset,
and of Irish Newfoundlanders

before flowing beyond identity
out past the Hook and into
the great embrace
of all waters —

the sister river deeply
past knowing or naming,
going on dying forever
while even yet springing

out of mossed earth
on a slope
in the Silvermine mountains
of north Tipperary

where glinting wetness
becomes a trickle,
a swelling,
a flowing

over and over,
old as the clouds
and young
as the hills.

Home

We share dark and light
with the Lesser Celandine
unveiling here its nothing
less than cosmic
gesture at our feet

for Earth has voyaged out
around its star again
with the valley and the river
and the wintered ground
where once more now

this little flower
rises from the clay
with modesty and grace
to proffer its small radiance
to the universe.

Notes

page 15 *The Three Sisters* having their confluence in Water-
and 155 ford Harbour: River Suir/*An tSiúir* (the sister); River
Nore/*An Fheoir* (meaning unknown); River Barrow/
An Bhearbha: (perhaps from Berba, a Tuatha Dé
Danann goddess). The poem 'Temair Lúachra'
(*Dinnseanchas*, ancient lore of places) has this refer-
ence in Old Irish:

> *In aidche rogéanair Conn*
> *ba fáillid ris Éire all,*
> *innti rochinnsetar tra*
> *Siúir, ocus Eóir, is Berba*

> . . . the night great Conn* was born,
> Éire showed her welcome
> by birthing that same night
> Suir, Nore and Barrow.

Conn Céadchathach: Conn of the Hundred Battles,
legendary king of Ireland and progenitor of the *Uí
Néill* dynasties.

page 24 The Gospel of St Mark, Chapter 5, opens with a
cluster of three compelling miracle stories. The third of
these describes the restoration to life of the daughter
of Jairus, ruler of the synagogue. When appealed to by
the child's father to save her Christ addresses the
girl in Aramaic, and in all Western translations of
this Gospel the phrase *Talitha cumi* survived in the
original language, with its meaning ('young maid,
arise') given.

page 68 James Clarence Mangan (1803-1849) satirized the
vanity of human possessions in his poem 'The Woman
of Three Cows' based on the anonymous Irish
original, 'Bean na dTrí mBó'.

page 78 *Aux Grands Hommes La Patrie Reconnaissante* (To
great men [from] a grateful homeland) reads the
epitaph above the neoclassical portico of the
Panthéon in Paris — France's national temple to its

most renowned citizens, the illustrious list including Voltaire, Rousseau, Victor Hugo and Émile Zola. Of seventy-four burials in the crypt, only two are women. Sophie Berthelot (1837-1907), having died of grief on the same day as her scientist husband Marcellin, was accorded the privilege of burial with him within the Panthéon 'in homage to her conjugal virtue' (Cell 25). Marie Curie, physicist, chemist and twice winner of the Nobel Prize, was reinterred in the Panthéon (Cell 8) in 1995 — to date the only woman so installed on her own merits.

Foucault's pendulum: Physicist Jean Bernard Léon Foucault (1819-1868) invented the pendulum device suspended by a wire 220 feet from the dome to the floor of the Panthéon. Its continuous arc of natural oscillation demonstrates the rotation of the Earth. In its time Foucault's invention was viewed as signifying the supremecy of scientific rationalism over religion.

page 90 *Oh play that thing*: traditional shout of encouragement in early jazz. 'The Duke': Edward Kennedy 'Duke' Ellington (1899-1973), American composer, pianist and bandleader.

page 100 Tatiana Rachevskaia was a Romanian student in Paris who took her own life, at the age of 23, in 1910 — reputedly under stress of a hopeless love for a doctor who was a friend of the sculptor Constantin Brancusi (1876-1957). Commissioned by the young woman's family, Brancusi carved a version of his famous sculpture 'Le Baiser' ('The Kiss') for her grave in Montparnasse Cemetery. Constantin Brancusi himself is also buried in Montparnasse, under an undecorated slab.

page 106 *La tristesse durera toujours.* / The sadness will last forever: one of the deathbed statements attributed to Vincent van Gogh by his brother Theo who was present at Vincent's death on 29th July 1890 at the Ravoux Inn in the village of Auvers-sur-Oise close to Paris. Vincent had inflicted a gunshot wound on himself in the local wheat fields on 27th July, dying as a result of it on the morning of the 29th. For years van

Gogh had carried on a voluminous correspondence with his brother, his artistic and financial supporter throughout his life. Theo died six months after Vincent and the brothers are buried side by side at Auvers-sur-Oise.

page 127 During the bloody Tudor campaigns in Munster six ships carrying Spanish, Italian and Irish soldiers left Spain in support of the rebel Earl of Desmond. When the force landed in November 1580 at Smerwick Harbour, County Kerry, it was besieged at Dún an Óir by overwhelming English forces on land and sea and surrendered after three days. An atrocity ensued in which 600 disarmed prisoners were butchered in cold blood on Lord Grey de Wilton's orders. Grey, Lord Lieutenant of Ireland, was accompanied at Dún an Óir by his secretary, the poet Edmund Spenser. The participation of Walter Raleigh in the massacre is claimed but disputed.

Local tradition records that the killing lasted two days in Gort a' Ghearradh (Field of the Cutting) and Gort na gCeann (Field of the Heads). The site now has a sculpture by Cliodna Cussen.

Kilmainham Jail, Dublin, is now a museum. The Stonebreakers' Yard there was the location for the executions of the court-martialled leaders of the 1916 Rising, shot in batches by the British military authorities during May of that year. This turned public opinion in favour of the rebels and significantly affected the subsequent course of modern Irish history as well as the hegemony of the British Empire. The Rising was the subject of Yeats's 'Easter 1916'.

page 132 Francis Scott Key Fitzgerald was born in St Paul, Minnesota, in 1896. He died suddenly of a heart attack in Hollywood in December 1940 and was interred at Rockville Union Cemetery, Rockville, Maryland, having been denied burial in the family plot at St Mary's there because he was deemed by local parish administrators not to be a practising Catholic. In 1948 his wife Zelda Sayre was buried at Union Cemetery with him when she died in a fire at a psychiatric hospital. Their daughter Scottie eventually overcame the original church burial ban and in 1975 Scott and Zelda's remains were reinterred together in the Fitzgerald family plot at St Mary's Church cemetery, to which their original headstone was also moved. Scottie in turn was buried there with them in 1986.

Acknowledgements

Versions of some of the foregoing work were broadcast on RTÉ Radio 1 and Lyric FM and published in *Captivating Brightness — Ballynahinch*, *The Cork Literary Review*, *Cyphers*, *The Echoing Years*, *Irish Pages*, *The Irish Times*, *New Hibernia Review*, *Poetry Ireland Review*, *The SHOp*, *Southword* and *The Stony Thursday Book*.

My thanks for support in general and particular ways to Aosdána (An Chomhairle Ealaíon/The Arts Council), to Poetry Ireland and, in respect of residencies, to James Murphy and the Department of Irish Studies, Villanova University, Pennsylvania, and Sheila Pratschke, Director, with the Board and staff of the Irish Cultural Centre, Paris. I am also deeply grateful to Brendan Flynn and Clifden Arts.

My wife Martina and our children Niamh, Lucy and James have been unfailingly supportive. I am fortunate in having the sustaining anchorage of community and friends. In relation to this book I remain especially indebted to Séamus McGrath, Tom Nealon, Pádraig Ó Macháin, Áine Ó Murchú, Dick and Brigid Meany, Rafa Alvarez, Jim Nolan and photographer John Crowley. I also thank the family of the late Helen Hickey, and express my particular appreciation of those most deeply connected with the river traditions of Carrick-on-Suir — especially the Power, Norris, O'Callaghan, Doherty, Fitzgerald, Robinson and McGrath families, in addition to Pat Drohan (cot builder and designer) and John Dwyer.

The fishermen in the cover photograph are Bobby Power, Anthony Robinson, Michael ('Mickser') Power and Michael ('Van Dyke') Power — the latter two also appear at the end of the book. I thank Ralph and William O'Callaghan for permission to publish my photograph of the river-borne funeral journey of their father, 'Willmo', who was a prime bearer of river tradition in the lower Suir valley.

My continuing gratitude is due to The Gallery Press and Jean and Peter Fallon with whom I have had a long and fruitful association over the years.